A Random House TELL ME ABOUT Book

DESERT ANIMALS

By Michael Chinery
Illustrated by Eric Robson
& David Wright

Random House 🏠 New York

First American edition, 1992.

Copyright © 1991 by Grisewood & Dempsey Ltd.
All rights reserved under International and Pan-American
Copyright Conventions. Published in the United States by
Random House, Inc., New York. Originally published in Great
Britain by Kingfisher Books, a Grisewood & Dempsey Company,
in 1991.

Library of Congress Cataloging in Publication Data
Chinery, Michael.
Desert animals / by Michael Chinery;
illustrated by David Wright and Eric Robson.
p. cm. — (A Random House tell me about book)
Includes index.
Summary: An introduction to the animals of the desert and how
they live, including the camel, jumping jerboa, and bearded
lizard.
ISBN 0-679-82048-5   ISBN 0-679-92048-X (lib. bdg.)
1. Desert fauna—Juvenile literature. [1. Desert animals.]
I. Wright, David, ill. II. Robson, Eric, ill. III. Title.
IV. Series.
QL116.C45   1992
591.909'54—dc20
91-53146

Manufactured in Hong Kong 1 2 3 4 5 6 7 8 9 10

Contents

Life in the deserts

Deserts are very dry places. They get less than 10 inches of rain every year. A year's rainfall may come in one tremendous storm lasting two or three days. Because the deserts are so dry for most of the year, the animals living there have to survive with very little water. The deserts are too hot for most animals in the daytime, so many of the desert animals come out at night.

DESERT FACTS

● Some deserts consist of mounds of sand called dunes. Others are composed of bare rocks or stones.

● The Atacama Desert in Chile can go for ten years without rain.

DO YOU KNOW

The southwestern desert, shown here, is full of cactus plants. One type, the giant saguaro, grows up to 60 feet high.

THE WORLD'S DESERTS

This map shows the world's deserts. Deserts are usually in the middle of continents. The winds have lost most of their moisture by the time they reach inland areas, and have little rain to drop. The southwestern U.S. is dry because the winds have dropped their water over the Rockies, a chain of mountains running right down the west coast of North America.

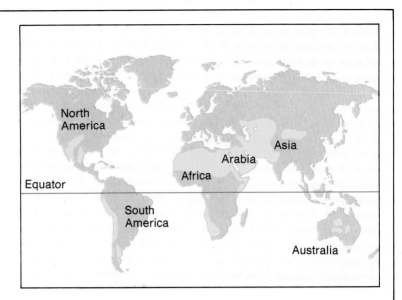

North America

Asia

Arabia

Africa

Equator

South America

Australia

The Arabian camel

There are two kinds of camel – the Arabian, with one hump, and the Bactrian, with two (page 8). Camels are perfectly designed for life in the dry, sandy deserts. An Arabian camel can live for several days without water, and can go for weeks without a drink if it has green plants to eat. The camel gets thin without water, but quickly returns to its usual weight after drinking. It can drink over 25 gallons in ten minutes!

Arabian camels roam the deserts of Arabia and North Africa in small groups. They eat the leaves of any trees and bushes they can find.

Long eyelashes shield the camel's eyes and protect them from the sand whipped up by the fierce desert winds.

The camel can close its nostrils between breaths so that the wind cannot blow sand up its nose.

The camel's hump is full of fat – a supply of food when food is hard to find. The hump shrinks as the food is gradually used up.

CAMEL FACTS

● The Arabian camel is about 10 feet long and nearly 7 feet high at the shoulder.

● Camels used for riding are a breed of Arabian camels called dromedaries. A good riding camel can travel over 90 miles a day.

Desert people have found all sorts of ways to use camels. They ride them, use them to carry goods, drink their milk, and burn their dried dung as fuel. Arabian camels have been taken to deserts in several other parts of the world.

Broad feet help to spread the camel's weight and stop it from sinking into the loose sand.

The Bactrian – a camel with two humps

Camels with two humps are called Bactrian camels. They live in the cold deserts of central Asia. Thick coats protect them from the cold. Like the one-humped camels of Arabia, they can go without food and water for long periods. Desert people domesticated, or tamed, the camels long ago so they could be used to carry goods and equipment.

BACTRIAN FACTS

● Bactrian camels are 7 feet high. They weigh about half a ton when fully grown.

● Domesticated camels have more hair than wild Bactrians. Camel hair is used to make blankets.

SURVIVAL WATCH

Truly wild Bactrian camels live only in the Gobi Desert in central Asia. Few are left now because people kill them for meat and leather. But there are still plenty of domesticated Bactrians.

People used to think that the humps carried water, but they actually contain stores of fat to keep the animals going when food is scarce.

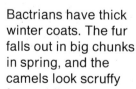

Bactrians have thick winter coats. The fur falls out in big chunks in spring, and the camels look scruffy for a while.

The cunning ant-lion

Not many animals make traps to catch their food, but a small insect called an ant-lion does. It digs cone-shaped pits in the sand, hides at the bottom, and waits for other insects to fall in. It is called an ant-lion because most of the insects that fall into its trap are ants.

Ant-lion pits may be up to 2 inches deep and 3 inches wide at the top. Where there are large groups of these pits it can be difficult for insects to avoid them.

Not all ant-lions make pits. Some bury themselves in the sand. When they sense that an insect is near, they rush out from their hiding place and grab it.

Ants lose their footing in the loose sand on the rim of the pit and start to slide down toward the waiting ant-lion.

When the ant-lion senses that an ant has tumbled into its pit, it flicks up sand to knock the insect within reach of its spiky jaws.

DO YOU KNOW

Ant-lions are actually young insects. When they mature, they turn into winged insects like the one shown below. The adult ant-lions feed on insects plucked from plants.

The fennec – a little fox with big ears

The fennec is the world's smallest fox, but it is the one with the biggest ears. The fennec uses its ears to listen for the faint sounds made by the animals that it hunts. It also listens for enemies, such as jackals and hyenas. The large ears also act like radiators to keep the fennec cool. Blood flows through them, just as water flows through a radiator, and gives off heat so that the animal does not get too hot.

DO YOU KNOW

Fennecs do not need to drink, even in the driest desert. They get all the water they need from their food.

Fennecs have become very popular pets.

FENNEC FACTS

● Fennecs live in the deserts of Africa and Arabia.

● The adult fennec's body is less than 16 inches long, but its ears are 6 inches long! Its bushy tail is about 10 inches long.

Fennecs avoid the hot sun by spending the daytime in burrows as much as 3 feet deep. The sand is much cooler there. The animals come out to hunt in the evening.

Insects and spiders make up much of the fennec's food, but sometimes these foxes eat larger animals, such as hares and gerbils.

The mother shows her cubs how to find food. When the cubs are born, their ears are short, but they soon grow quickly.

The kit fox – a fennec look-alike

The kit fox lives in the American Southwest, a long way from the fennec's African home. But the two animals look alike and share similar lifestyles. The kit fox spends the daytime in a deep burrow where the air is cool. It comes out at nightfall to hunt for small animals and picks up their sounds with its huge ears. The kit fox dashes after the animals at high speed and carries them back to its burrow to eat them.

SURVIVAL WATCH

Kit foxes are becoming rare. Many have been killed by poison intended for coyotes. Their homes are also being destroyed as towns spread into the desert.

Huge ears help the kit fox to stay cool. They also pick up every sound in the desert at night as the animal hunts for food.

Kit foxes eat all kinds of small animals, including rabbits and lizards. This kangaroo rat is about to become the fox's next meal.

KIT FOX FACTS

● Kit foxes live on the grassy plains as well as in the desert.

● The kit fox is about 3 feet long, including its bushy tail. It is also called the swift fox because it can run very fast.

The speedy oryx

Oryx are fast-running antelope found in the deserts of Africa and Arabia. The Arabian oryx pictured here is the smallest and rarest of the three different kinds. It lives in small herds in a few parts of the Arabian Desert and feeds on scattered clumps of grass, usually early in the morning, when there is some dew to provide extra moisture.

Oryx herds gallop away when alarmed, but if the animals are cornered, they put their heads down and attack with their long, sharp horns.

SURVIVAL WATCH

The Arabian oryx almost died out in the 1960s. Fortunately, zoos have been able to breed them, but there may no longer be any oryx left in the wild.

The horns of the Arabian oryx are about 30 inches long and almost straight. When seen from the side, the animal appears to have only one horn.

ORYX FACTS

Oryx herds consist mainly of females and their young. Most adult males live by themselves and join the herds only in the mating season.

The addax

The addax is a sturdy antelope that lives in some of the driest parts of the Sahara Desert. Small herds wander from place to place looking for fresh grass. Fresh leaves grow quickly after brief showers, and the addax has a wonderful ability to smell the new leaves from a distance. Addaxes can go without water for long periods, and some of them probably never drink at all. They get all the water they need from the grass.

SURVIVAL WATCH

The addax used to be common in the deserts of North Africa and Arabia, but it is now rare because people hunt it for its skin and its long spiral horns. Herds of goats which graze in the desert also threaten the addax by eating the grass that the addax needs.

The addax is 3 feet high at the shoulder. Its coat is grayish in winter and white or sandy in the summer.

Broad hooves enable the addax to walk or run easily over loose sand without sinking into it.

13

The jumping jerboa

Jerboas are built for jumping. They bound along on their long back legs like miniature kangaroos. Several kinds of jerboas live in the deserts of Africa and Asia. Like most small desert animals, they hide in underground burrows during the day and come out to feed at night. Jerboas feed mainly on seeds and leaves, but they also eat beetles and other insects. They use their short front legs for picking up food.

JERBOA FACTS

● Jerboas have excellent hearing and eyesight and a superb sense of smell.

● Jerboas are able to leap 3 feet or more into bushes to grab juicy leaves.

Even in its burrow the jerboa is not always safe from its enemies. Sometimes a snake will slither inside in search of a meal.

The jerboa's hind legs are four times as long as its front legs and enable it to travel in huge leaps of up to 10 feet at a time.

As soon as the jerboa realizes that it is in danger, it explodes out of the other end of the tunnel in a spray of sand.

The kangaroo rat

The kangaroo rat is the American equivalent of the jerboa. It looks like a tiny kangaroo as it leaps over the desert floor at night. Its main enemies are owls and snakes. The kangaroo rat feeds mainly on grass and seeds.

? DO YOU KNOW

Kangaroo rats often spread from the deserts to farmland, where they do a lot of damage by digging up newly planted crops.

The Mongolian gerbil

The Mongolian gerbil, also known as a jird, comes from the deserts of central Asia. It lives in huge colonies and is active both day and night. If alarmed, the gerbil warns its neighbors by thumping the ground with its big hind feet.

? DO YOU KNOW

Gerbils make fine pets. They love to sit up and look around—just as they do when looking out for danger in the wild. Pet gerbils can live for up to five years.

Gerbils hold their food in their tiny front paws. The Mongolian gerbil has long back legs but is not a good jumper.

The dainty dorcas gazelle

This small antelope is only 2 feet high at the shoulder, but it can run at 50 mph (miles per hour). It lives in the dry grasslands and deserts that stretch from West Africa to India. It feeds on roots and leaves and gets most of the water it needs from this food.

The dorcas gazelle is also called the jebeer. It is a rare animal and is in great danger of extinction in all of the areas where it lives.

DO YOU KNOW

In North Africa the dorcas gazelle is pale brown with straight horns, but in India it has a rich brown coat and its horns are more curved.

The wild ass – a desert donkey

Wild asses live in Africa and Asia. They can survive for many days without drinking, but when they do find water, they can drink over 10 gallons in just a few minutes. These animals were the ancestors of our domestic donkeys.

SURVIVAL WATCH

Only a few wild asses survive in Asia. In Africa there are probably no wild asses left at all. The asses that do live there are almost certainly donkeys that have gone wild.

Piles of rocks can offer welcome shade from the scorching heat of the sun.

Squabbling ground squirrels

Not all squirrels live in trees. Ground squirrels live in burrows in the ground. Several kinds are found in the hot deserts of California and South Africa. They can stand higher temperatures than most other small mammals and are active during the daytime, but they still need shelter from the midday sun. Ground squirrels live in colonies, and hundreds of animals may share a network of tunnels.

DO YOU KNOW

Squirrel tails have many uses. Tree squirrels use them to help change direction, while many ground squirrels use them for signaling. Squirrels in cold areas wrap their tails around their bodies to keep warm, and desert squirrels use their tails as sunshades.

During the daytime ground squirrels sit with their backs to the sun and keep cool by using their bushy tails as sunshades.

DO YOU KNOW

Desert-living ground squirrels feed mainly on seeds and insects.

Ground squirrels often squabble during the morning and evening. It is too hot to fight in the middle of the day.

When the desert gets too hot, the squirrels look for shade. They go into their burrows or hide among rocks, where they cool down quickly.

The sand grouse – a flying water carrier

The sand grouse is an expert in desert survival. It nests in the stony deserts of Africa and Asia and can raise a family in much drier places than other birds. Its secret is that the male birds use their fluffy breast feathers like sponges to soak up water and carry it back to their chicks. Some birds fly over 60 miles every day just to find water and take it back to their nests.

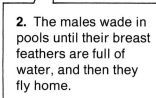

1. Sand grouse are fast fliers. The flocks of males often make a lot of noise as they fly to the water holes.

2. The males wade in pools until their breast feathers are full of water, and then they fly home.

3. When the sand grouse returns to his nest, his chicks suck the water from his soggy feathers.

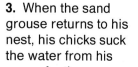

SAND GROUSE FACTS

● Sand grouse usually fly to the water holes early in the morning. They may go back again at dusk. They set off and return at almost the same time every day.

● Sand-colored feathers give good desert camouflage.

The ferocious camel spider

For its size, the camel spider has some of the most powerful jaws in the whole animal world. And it has an appetite to match. It will go on eating until it is so full that it can hardly move. A single camel spider can eat over 100 small flies in 24 hours. Camel spiders feed mainly on insects, including tough-skinned beetles, but they will also eat scorpions, lizards, and even small birds.

CAMEL SPIDER FACTS

● Camel spiders live mainly in the deserts of Africa and Asia.

● These animals are up to 2 inches long. They run quickly and are often mistaken for mice.

● Camel spiders are also called wind scorpions or sun spiders, even though most of them are active only at night.

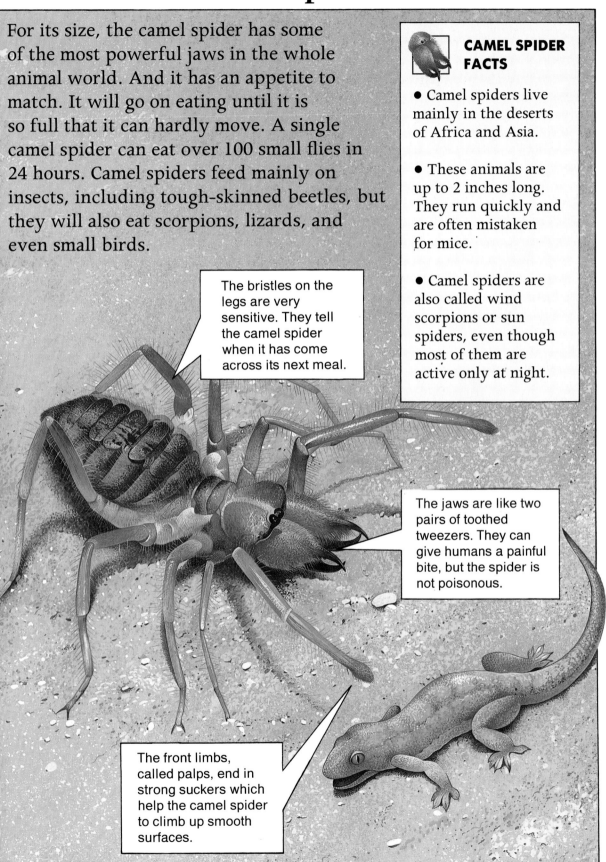

The bristles on the legs are very sensitive. They tell the camel spider when it has come across its next meal.

The jaws are like two pairs of toothed tweezers. They can give humans a painful bite, but the spider is not poisonous.

The front limbs, called palps, end in strong suckers which help the camel spider to climb up smooth surfaces.

The dancing scorpion

You can recognize a scorpion by its big claws and its slender tail. The tail has a sting on the end and is usually curled forward. Some scorpions can kill people with their stings, but they do not usually sting unless they are annoyed. Most scorpions live in hot areas, and many kinds live in the deserts. At night they walk slowly in search of food. Insects and spiders are their main foods, but large scorpions also eat lizards and mice.

SCORPION FACTS

● There are about 650 different kinds of scorpions. The biggest are about 8 inches long. Only a few are really dangerous.

● Some scorpions can survive without food for over a year.

● Scorpions have been known to survive being frozen in ice for several weeks.

Courting scorpions go dancing. The male holds his partner with his claws and the two animals move jerkily around until they are ready to mate. Males who do not dance properly may well get stung.

With its small eyes, the scorpion cannot see very well. It relies mainly on touch and smell to learn what is going on around it.

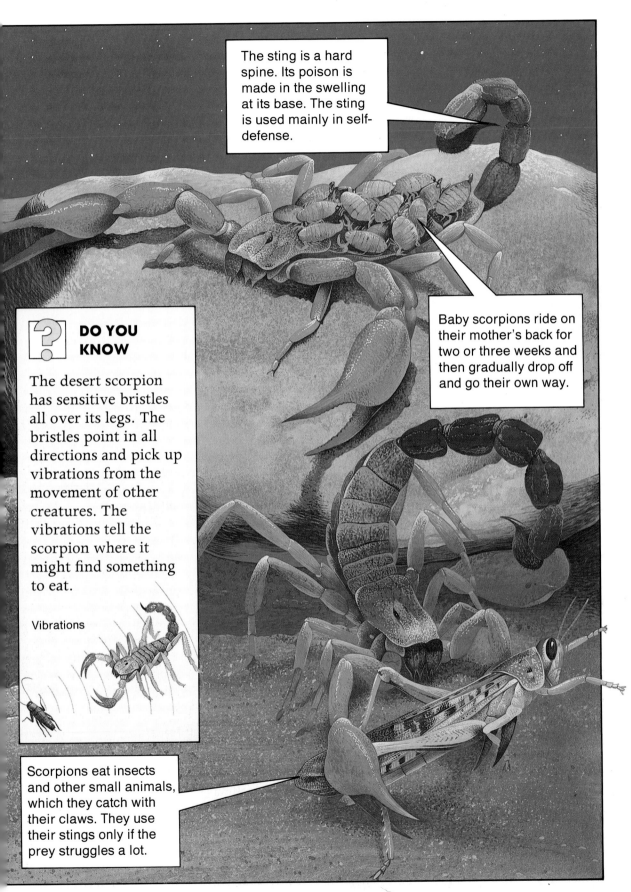

The sting is a hard spine. Its poison is made in the swelling at its base. The sting is used mainly in self-defense.

Baby scorpions ride on their mother's back for two or three weeks and then gradually drop off and go their own way.

? DO YOU KNOW

The desert scorpion has sensitive bristles all over its legs. The bristles point in all directions and pick up vibrations from the movement of other creatures. The vibrations tell the scorpion where it might find something to eat.

Vibrations

Scorpions eat insects and other small animals, which they catch with their claws. They use their stings only if the prey struggles a lot.

The sand cat

Sand cats live in the deserts of North Africa and Arabia. Their yellowish or grayish brown fur helps to camouflage them against the sand as they stalk their prey.

Hairy soles give the sand cat's feet a good grip on the loose desert sand.

The head is broad and flat, so the cat can peer out from behind small rocks.

The golden mole

Golden moles look like balls of silky fur. They spend most of their time "swimming" through the sand, pushing up ridges wherever they go. They are found only in southern Africa, and they feed mainly on insects and lizards.

A tough pad of skin protects the mole's nostrils while it is burrowing. Its legs are so short that you can hardly see them.

DO YOU KNOW

The golden mole's eyes and ears are covered with skin. The animal finds its food by picking up scents and vibrations.

Although it is a tiny animal, just 3 inches long, the golden mole can travel over 2 miles in a single night.

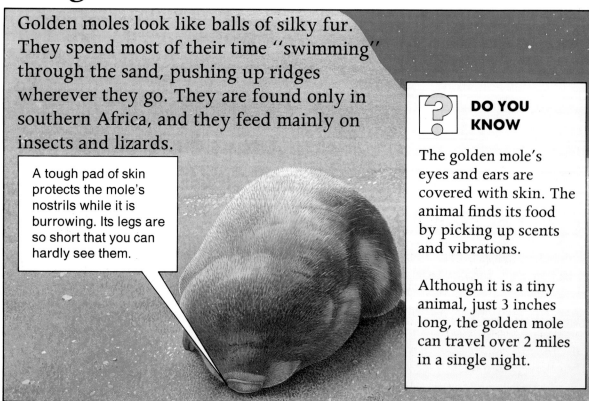

The caracal – a high-flying cat

The caracal is one of the world's fastest cats. It catches hares and small antelope. It can also charge at a flock of birds and catch several of them before they can fly away. And the birds are not safe even if they do manage to take off, because the caracal can leap into the air and catch them. Even eagles can be caught by this amazing cat. Caracals live around the edges of the deserts of Africa, Arabia, and India.

The caracal has long legs and is a superb high jumper. It can leap $6\frac{1}{2}$ feet into the air to take birds by surprise.

Powerful paws can kill a bird with one blow, knocking it to the ground or sweeping it straight into the caracal's mouth.

CARACAL FACTS

- The caracal is about 2 feet long and up to 18 inches high at the shoulder. It weighs up to 35 pounds.

- Caracals can run at more than 30 mph over short distances.

23

The bearded lizard

The bearded lizard, also called the bearded dragon, is named for the bristly shield on its throat. It is about 2 feet long and lives in the Australian deserts. It spends a lot of time basking in the late afternoon sunshine. This keeps its body warm through the evening, so it can go on looking for food long after other lizards have cooled down and gone to sleep. It feeds mainly on insects.

DO YOU KNOW

The bearded lizard can run on its hind legs. This helps to cool its body by lifting it clear of the hot ground.

On hot ground, the lizard often cools its feet by lifting each foot in turn.

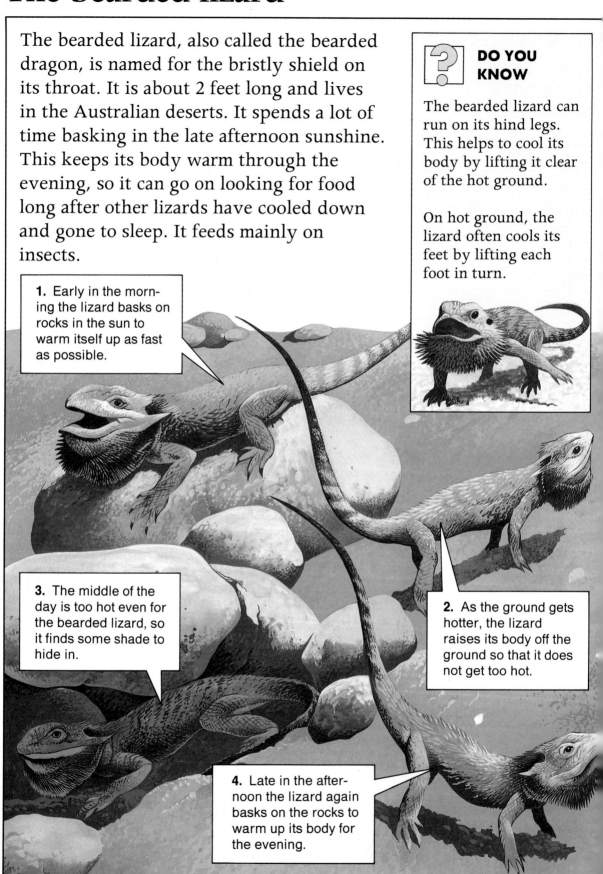

1. Early in the morning the lizard basks on rocks in the sun to warm itself up as fast as possible.

3. The middle of the day is too hot even for the bearded lizard, so it finds some shade to hide in.

2. As the ground gets hotter, the lizard raises its body off the ground so that it does not get too hot.

4. Late in the afternoon the lizard again basks on the rocks to warm up its body for the evening.

The spadefoot toad

Many people are amazed to learn that there are toads in the deserts, because toads have to grow up in water. The toads pictured here are American spadefoots. Their lives seem to be speeded up to fit in with the desert's short rainy season. They are called spadefoots because their back legs have spadelike blades used for digging burrows.

As soon as the rainy season arrives, the spadefoot toads leave their burrows and mate. The females lay strings of eggs.

The eggs hatch in just two days, and the tadpoles eat quickly. It's a race against time, because the pools will soon dry up.

After about two weeks the tadpoles turn into tiny toads. They hop away from the pools, which are already almost dry.

The toads spend up to ten months of the year in deep burrows, which they dig with the broad blades on their back feet.

? DO YOU KNOW

Some spadefoot tadpoles eat tiny plants. Others eat their brothers and sisters. These cannibals grow quickly and may live even if the pools dry up in a few days.

The thorny devil

The thorny devil is a slow-moving lizard from the sandy deserts of Australia. It does not need to move quickly, because it is protected from attack by its spines. Dew forming on the lizard's spines at night provides it with drinking water.

THORNY DEVIL FACTS

- The thorny devil is about 6 inches long.

- The devil can pick up 40 ants in a minute and eat 1,000 ants in a single meal.

The frilled lizard

The frilled lizard is a phony. When it is frightened, it spreads the skin on its neck and pretends to be much bigger and fiercer than it really is. This display scares away its enemies. Frilled lizards live in the deserts and dry grasslands of Australia.

The frill contains stiff rods, like an umbrella. The lizard makes a loud hissing noise, which makes it seem even fiercer.

The poisonous Gila monster

This plump, slow-moving lizard lives in the deserts of North America. Its bite is poisonous, and its bright colors warn other animals to leave it alone. It feeds mainly on birds' eggs and other small animals.

GILA MONSTER FACTS

● The Gila monster is up to 2 feet long and is active mainly in the wet season.

● This rare animal is now protected by law.

The lizard stores food in its fat tail. The food keeps the lizard going through the dry season.

Like most lizards, the monster tracks down its food by flicking its tongue out to pick up the scent of its prey.

The chuckwalla

Chuckwalla lizards live in North America's rocky deserts. They eat the desert flowers in spring and early summer and sleep for the rest of the year. If alarmed, the lizard dives into a rock crevice and pumps its body up with air so that it cannot be pulled out.

CHUCKWALLA FACTS

● The chuckwalla is 18 inches long and weighs about $3\frac{1}{2}$ pounds.

● It sleeps for seven months of the year.

Deadly desert rattlesnakes

Several kinds of rattlesnakes, or rattlers, live in the deserts of North America. They get their name from the rattling or hissing noise they make with their tails when they are disturbed. The rattle warns larger animals to keep away, for the snake does not want to waste its poison on animals too large for it to eat. It feeds at night on rabbits and other small mammals. Although their bite is poisonous, rattlesnakes are eaten by other snakes, by a bird called the roadrunner, and by people.

DO YOU KNOW

A rattlesnake can track down its prey in total darkness with the aid of a heat-sensitive pit on each side of its head. Nerves in these pits pick up the warmth of the prey and tell the snake exactly where the prey is to be found.

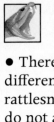

RATTLESNAKE FACTS

● There are about 30 different kinds of rattlesnakes, but they do not all live in the deserts. The biggest rattlesnakes are over 6 feet long.

Heat-sensitive pits on its head tell the rattlesnake when it is getting close to its warm-blooded prey.

SIDEWINDER TRACKS

The small sidewinder rattlesnake has a clever way of moving over loose sand. It throws its body into loops and almost rolls along. Only two points of its body touch the ground at any one time, leaving parallel tracks in the sand.

The fangs swing forward when the snake opens its mouth, ready to strike, and inject deadly poison into the prey.

Each time a rattler changes its skin, it adds a new ring to its rattle. This means that the rattle gets bigger and louder as the snake grows older.

The pack rat

The pack rat of the Southwest spends much of its life scampering over prickly cacti, so it has to be careful where it puts its feet. It nests in cactus clumps and protects the nest by piling other pieces of cactus around it. There are several grass-lined rooms in the nest, and the pack rat sleeps in one of them during the day.

PACK RAT FACTS

● The pack rat is not really a rat but a vole. It is about 18 inches long including its tail.

● Pack rats like shiny coins and other bright objects. They collect them and store them in their nests.

Pack rats get all the water they need from the juicy stems and fruits of the cacti. They sometimes eat small insects.

The nest entrance is just wide enough for the pack rat. Enemies such as the kit fox cannot get into the prickly nest.

The long-eared jack rabbit

Jack rabbits are actually hares. They have much longer legs and ears than true rabbits. Several kinds live in North America. The black-tailed jack rabbit pictured here lives in the deserts. It does not burrow and avoids the daytime heat by sitting in the shade of a cactus or a rock. Its huge ears help it to keep cool.

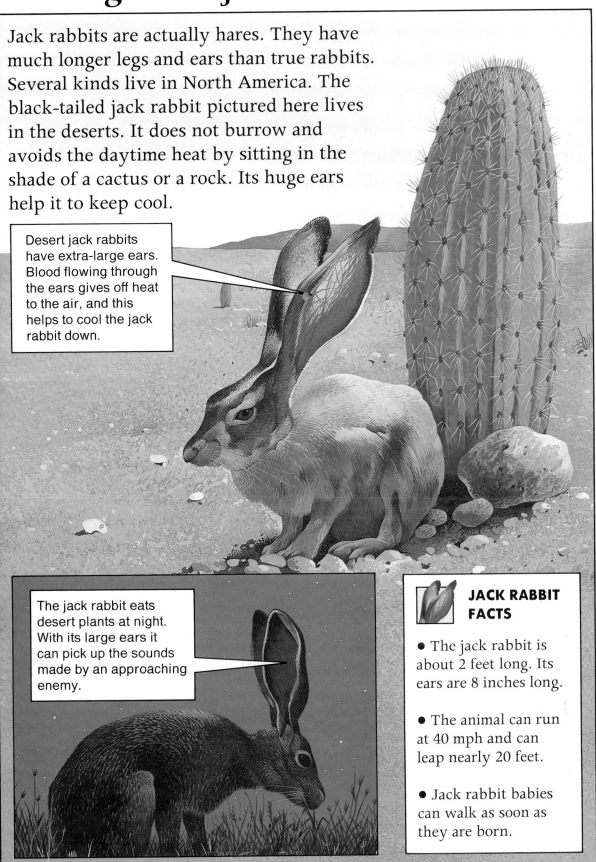

Desert jack rabbits have extra-large ears. Blood flowing through the ears gives off heat to the air, and this helps to cool the jack rabbit down.

The jack rabbit eats desert plants at night. With its large ears it can pick up the sounds made by an approaching enemy.

JACK RABBIT FACTS

● The jack rabbit is about 2 feet long. Its ears are 8 inches long.

● The animal can run at 40 mph and can leap nearly 20 feet.

● Jack rabbit babies can walk as soon as they are born.

The Gila woodpecker

There are not many trees in the desert, so the Gila woodpecker has to make do with the tree-shaped giant saguaro cacti. Saguaro cacti grow to about 50 feet high in the Southwest and provide food and shelter for many animals. The Gila woodpecker feeds mainly on beetles and other insects living in the saguaro's juicy stems. It nests in neat, round holes which it digs in the stems with its sturdy beak.

SURVIVAL WATCH

The Gila woodpecker has few enemies and is not in any direct danger, but its home is under threat. The saguaro cactus, which takes about 200 years to reach its full size, is dying out in some of the desert areas.

DO YOU KNOW

You can tell a male Gila woodpecker from a female because only the male has a red cap.

The wounded flesh of the nest hole forms a sort of scab and becomes dry, so the hole makes a comfortable nest for the woodpecker and its chicks. Few enemies can reach the nest.

The Gila woodpecker supports itself with its stiff tail feathers while clinging to the stem of the cactus.

Backward and forward facing toes give the woodpecker's clawed feet a really secure grip on the side of the saguaro.

The elf owl

Elf owls live in the southwestern deserts, especially in areas where the saguaro cacti grow. The birds fly at night and spend the daytime resting in holes in the cacti. They usually use old woodpecker nests.

The large eyes of the elf owl help the bird to see its insect prey in the dark.

ELF OWL FACTS

- The elf owl is only about 5 inches long and is one of the world's smallest owls. It feeds on insects, spiders, and scorpions.

The burrowing owl

Burrowing owls live on the plains and in the deserts of North America. They fly by day and spend the night in underground burrows. They can dig their own holes, but they prefer burrows dug by other animals.

Burrowing owls are about 8 inches long and have longer legs than most other owls. They eat insects and other small animals.

SURVIVAL WATCH

Burrowing owls are now rare on the plains because farming destroys their nests. And in the deserts they are at risk from the spread of towns.

The remarkable roadrunner

The roadrunner lives in some of the hottest parts of the American Southwest. It has short wings and does not fly very much. The bird is 20–24 inches long and feeds mainly on insects and scorpions. It also catches lizards and snakes and crushes them with its strong feet before eating them. The roadrunner hunts early in the morning and in the evening. It keeps cool in the middle of the day by sitting in the shade of rocks.

DO YOU KNOW

The roadrunner is a member of the cuckoo family. It got its name from its habit of running next to horse-drawn wagons and eating the insects disturbed by the horses' hooves.

The roadrunner usually runs at about 15 mph, but it has a top speed of 25 mph. It uses its wings to keeps its balance.

The roadrunner often builds its nest in cactus bushes, where it is safe from most of its enemies. It lays up to six eggs.

The mourning dove

Mourning doves can live in extremely hot and dry conditions and sometimes nest in the hottest parts of the American Southwest. But they still need water and may fly 60 miles or more every day to drink. These birds also live in cities and on farmland.

Mourning doves often nest on prickly cacti. They do not seem to mind the sun's heat beating down on them.

MOURNING DOVE FACTS

● The mourning dove is about 10 inches long and is a fast flier.

● The dove is named for its sad, cooing call. Its wings make a whistling sound in flight.

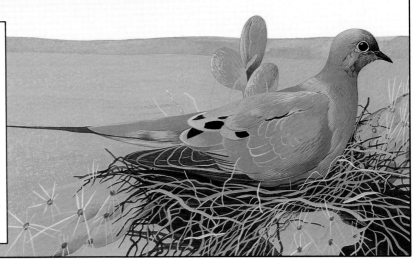

The desert tortoise

Desert tortoises are up to 14 inches long and live in the American Southwest. They feed mainly on cacti. As long as they have juicy cacti to eat, they do not need to drink, even in the dry season. They store water from the cacti in their bodies.

SURVIVAL WATCH

Desert tortoises are now rare because thousands have been collected and sold as pets. Laws now protect these animals, so they may increase again in the wild.

Tortoises have sharp-edged horny jaws instead of teeth. These tough jaws can munch through prickly cacti without harm.

Harvester ants

Harvester ants live in many of the drier parts of the world and feed mainly on seeds. Worker ants stream out from their nests every day and bring back seeds from as far as 300 feet away. Large-headed workers, often called soldiers, crack the seeds open with their strong jaws. The soft kernels are stored in special chambers in the nest. The husks are thrown out and often form a large mound around the nest entrance.

DO YOU KNOW

The ants in each nest collect millions of seeds in a year, mostly at the end of the wet season. The stored seeds keep the ants alive through the dry season, when food is scarce. The seeds do not sprout in the nest because it is too dry.

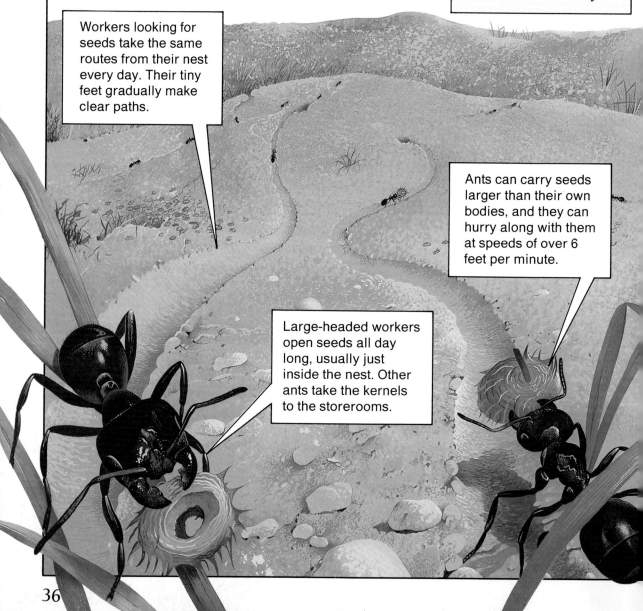

Workers looking for seeds take the same routes from their nest every day. Their tiny feet gradually make clear paths.

Ants can carry seeds larger than their own bodies, and they can hurry along with them at speeds of over 6 feet per minute.

Large-headed workers open seeds all day long, usually just inside the nest. Other ants take the kernels to the storerooms.

Honeypot ants

Honeypot ants live in the North American and Australian deserts and feed mainly on nectar from flowers. Since the flowers bloom only for a short time after it rains, the ants have developed a way of storing the nectar for use in the dry season. Some of the ants in the colony turn themselves into living "honeypots." Workers pass nectar to the honeypots, whose bodies gradually swell up. In the dry season, when the other ants are hungry, the honeypots feed them with the nectar.

The honeypots start to fill up with nectar as soon as they have grown up, while their skins are still soft and stretchy. Some kinds of honeypot ants store fruit juices instead of nectar.

A worker returning to the nest passes its load of nectar to one of the honeypots for safekeeping.

Honeypot ants make their nests deep in the ground, sometimes as much as 6 feet below the surface.

The honeypot cannot move and spends all its life hanging from the roof of the nest. It is about as big as a pea when full.

 DO YOU KNOW

Honeypot nests may contain 1,500 living honeypots, all bulging with sweet nectar.

Australian Aborigines – the native people of Australia – dig up the honeypots and eat them like candy.

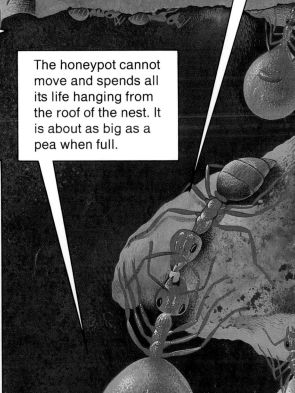

Deserts in danger

Deserts are harsh places, and few people live in them. Even so, we are still damaging many deserts. Farms and towns are spreading into the American Southwest, thanks to huge irrigation systems that bring water to the dry areas. Mining is being done in many areas to extract valuable minerals. Much of the world's oil lies under the deserts, especially in the Middle East, and oil wells cover thousands of acres of desert.

BRAND-NEW DESERTS

Some deserts are actually growing, especially in parts of Africa. A decrease in rainfall in these areas is one reason for this. People are also to blame. They let too many sheep and goats graze on the thin grass. The plants are killed and the wind blows the topsoil away. All that is left is a dry, dusty landscape – a desert. In a dry climate it does not take long to turn grassland and woodland into desert.

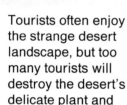

Tourists often enjoy the strange desert landscape, but too many tourists will destroy the desert's delicate plant and animal life.

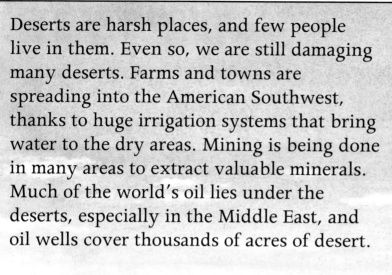

Useful words

Bask   To warm up the body by sitting in the heat of the sun.

Cactus   Any of the many spiny plants of the American Southwest. Their leafless stems, which are like barrels or pipes, are used to store water. As the water is used up during the dry season, the stems shrink and become deeply grooved. The plural of cactus is cacti.

Camouflage   To color something so that it is not easily seen, especially by an enemy. Animals use many forms of camouflage to trick their enemies. Some use camouflage to avoid being caught, while others use it to take their prey by surprise.

Colony   A group of animals that live closely together and help each other. Each member of the colony usually has a particular job.

Desert   A region that receives less than 10 inches of rain in a year. The deserts cover about one seventh of the earth's land area. The biggest desert is the Sahara, in North Africa. It covers about $3\frac{1}{2}$ million square miles – nearly as much as the entire United States of America.

Dew   Water produced from moisture in the air when the air cools down at night. Cold air cannot hold as much moisture as warm air, so it drops the moisture as dew on the ground and on low-growing plants.

Domestic   Not wild. Domesticated animals have been tamed by people for various purposes.

Extinction   The dying out of any kind of plant or animal. An extinct creature is one that no longer lives anywhere on earth.

Fangs   The large teeth of a snake that inject poison into its prey.

Herd   The name given to any large group of hoofed animals, such as antelope, that live and feed together.

Husk   The tough, outer coat of a seed.

Insect   A small animal with six legs and a body that has three sections. Ant-lions and ants are insects, but spiders and scorpions, which have eight legs, are not.

Kernel   The soft, inner part of a seed, which grows into a new plant.

Mammal   Any animal that feeds its babies with milk from the mother's body. Several types of mammals live in the deserts, from the tiny kangaroo rat to the much larger camel.

Nature reserve   An area set aside to protect wild plants and animals – often rare ones that are in danger of dying out.

Prey   Any animal that is caught and eaten by another animal. Animals that hunt for prey are called predators.

Stalk   To creep up on something – usually prey – slowly and silently.

Tadpole   The young stage in the life of a frog or toad. Tadpoles live in water, but they grow up to become air-breathing animals living out of the water.

Vibration   A movement of the air or ground, often caused by something moving nearby.

Water hole   A pond where animals regularly gather to drink.

Index